Why?

Why?

reflections on the loss of a loved one

by Rabbi Yitzchak Vorst

FELDHEIM PUBLISHERS
Jerusalem / New York

Translated from the Dutch
Overpeinzingen — Over pijn zingen

Edited by Charles Wengrov

First published 1990.

Second, revised edition 1990.

Paperback edition: ISBN 0-87306-525-5

Distributed by:

Philipp Feldheim, Inc.
200 Airport Executive Park
Spring Valley, NY 10977

Feldheim Publishers, Ltd.
POB 6525 / Jerusalem, Israel

Printed in Israel

Contents

Foreword

"Just as God comforted mourners... so shall you too comfort mourners."

This small book is an attempt that I have made to obey this kindly, humane instruction of our Talmudic Sages —to reach out through the written word and offer solace and comfort to others who, like myself, have suffered bereavement.

These pages were written, from my own chassidic viewpoint, while I was in mourning over the death of someone I loved. They are presented here in the hope that, if (may Heaven forbid) someone has suffered a tragic loss, the thoughts and feelings expressed in this little book may help him through it. May it offer him some help and support in the difficult days that he will have to face.

I

Work ran late tonight. At a meeting with the other members of the Amstelveen committee, we prepared the material for the next issue of *Baderech*, for the periodical of the Jewish community of Amsterdam-Amstelveen. With God's help, it will be a good issue. It deals with washing the hands before a meal, the *b*e*racha* over the bread, the Shabbat meal, and the recall of the manna in the wilderness. I think we have expressed rather well the concept that manna is the food which shows us trust in God:

What is the deeper meaning of the fact that we remember the manna on Shabbat?

Imagine that you are in the wilderness of Sinai, 3300 years ago. You are there together with two or three million others. There must be food and water. And then, fortunately, each and every day food descends— miraculously. There is enough for everybody. But nothing may be kept until the next day. You must demonstrate your trust in God, your faith that He will see to it that tomorrow there will be food again...in the dry, barren wilderness...for two or three million people! Manna is the food of trust in God. And years later, when the Prophet Yirme yahu was confronted by the complaint of the Jewish people that they could not devote themselves to study of the Torah, for "who shall provide us with our daily bread?"—he showed them a little jar with manna, which had been kept at God's command (Exodus 16:33)—and he said: "Look at the word of God, see the manna! God can provide for us in many ways."

This thought of trust in God remains relevant for us every Shabbat again, when we abandon our business, our work. For He can provide for us in so many ways.

In this issue of *Baderech*, we considered it important to include the translation of a prayer which expresses the thought that it is God who provides for everyone and everything. It is He who gives us *banei, hayyei um^ezonei* — children, health and our daily needs.

*

At the end of the issue comes a story out of our past, and of the rich history of our people. We tell about Reb Pesach, one of the Ḥassidim of Rabbi Shmuel Schneerson, the fourth Lubavitcher Rebbe:

One of the Ḥassidim of Rabbi Shmuel was an illiterate man named Reb Pesach. He made a living by traveling with all kinds of merchandise from the town of Homiel to the surrounding villages, to sell it there to the shopkeepers.

For Rosh Hashana 5627 (1866) he came to stay with Rabbi Shmuel; and the Rebbe welcomed him with the words, "You can always fulfill the command S^e'u marom eineichem; sh^ema—*that is Yisrael."*

*One of the other Ḥassidim explained to Reb Pesach what Rabbi Shmuel meant: "The high windows in the shul are there not only to let the light enter, but also to make it possible for us to lift up our eyes unto high—*s^e'u marom eineichem. *When we lift up our eyes to heaven, we learn to honor God. But you—not only in shul (the synagogue), but also at work—you can lift up your eyes. Thus you can always observe the command* S^e'u marom eineichem—*whose first letters form the word* sh^ema. *After this word comes the word* Yisrael. *By saying and experiencing the words of* sh^ema, *you can reach the level of Yisrael, the name of honor of the Jewish people."*

These words made a deep impression on Reb Pesach. With the help of his neighbor, the watchmaker Reb Hirschl, he began to study Torah little by little, and he became a warm, lebediker *(enthusiastic) Jew.*

In 1928, when he was about ninety years old, Reb Pesach said:

It is now sixty-two years since the Rebbe blessed me with those words: S^e'u marom eineichem; sh^ema—*that is Yisrael. Every day since then, whenever I say* sh^ema Yisrael, *I have this in mind. God grant that when my* *time comes, my mind will still be clear enough to know it: sh^ema — that is Yisrael.*

It is too late to go to shul, and I say my morning prayers at home. That happens from time to time, as it is not easy for my wife to take care of the children in the morning all by herself. We have six children, and are expecting the seventh. We love children. We find nothing strange or wrong in having a large family, for my wife and I are both from families with many children. It is only natural for us, since Jewish law allows birth control only in an emergency. Children are a blessing from God—may we always be aware of that—and the more blessing from God the better. Moreover, in the aftermath of the Holocaust, the Jewish people certainly need very many children.

*

The four oldest of our brood have gone off to school. Boruch, our three-year-old son, snuggles against me on the couch. He is a lovely boy, gentle and sweet. We are all fond of him. I pull him closer and begin to pray. I sing a penetrating chassidic melody which I have often heard Ḥassidim of the Lubavitcher Rebbe sing while they wait for him to appear. It is a melody without set words; but now I sing the words of *Lokeil boruch* to it.

Lokeil	*To God,*
boruch	*the Blessed One (Who lets Himself be drawn close to His world)*

n^e'imot yitenu	*they chant pleasant melodies.*
l^emelech	*For the King,*
keil ḥai v^ekayam	*the ever living and existing God,*
z^emirot yomeiru	*they sound sweet hymns*
v^etishbaḥot yashmi'u	*and sound songs of praise.*
	(What concepts are expressed in these songs and hymns?)
Ki hu levado	*He alone is (God alone exists. His existence is* true *existence:*
	m^etsi'uto me'atsmuto: His existence is inherent from Himself, from His essential being. The worlds are manifestations of God. The worlds exist "in" God, and are forever dependent on Him. They have no existence of their own.)
marom v^ekadosh	*He is sublime and holy (on the one hand God is supremely* **above** *the world,* **above** *creation, but at the same time it is He—and He alone)*
po'eil g^evurot	*Who performs mighty deeds* **in** *the world*
oseh ḥadashot	*He makes new things*
ba'al milḥamot	*He is the Lord of wars*
zorei'a ts^edakot	*He sows acts of charity*
matsmi-aḥ y^eshu'ot	*He makes salvation grow.*

While the melody still sings within me, I reflect on these words. What do the terms "sow" and "make grow" mean in connection with charity and salvation?

Chabad Chassidism explains that "to make salvation grow" refers to Divine help which comes after a situation that **we** experience as negative but which is actually an **intermediate**, **transitory phase**, a "passing-through" period, that was a necessary **preparation** for a later, glorious situation.

It is beyond our power to see this process as it is planned by God, from the start. At best we can understand it afterwards, in retrospect.

I once heard an amusing parable which is perhaps not entirely accurate from the scientific point of view, but which clearly illustrates this concept of "making grow" (causing growth). We included this "Parable of the Worm" in *Baderech:*

Once there was a worm. True to his nature, he dug a way through the soil in search of food for himself and his family—and Father worm was lucky: he found a beautiful, perfect potato. Quickly (or as quickly as a worm can go) he returned home and told his wife and children of the precious treasure he had found. But alas, his emotions overcame him: the excitement and the exertion were too much for him, and he died.

Now his son began to search for the potato, for he was now the legal heir to it. He crawled along and found it, but great was his disappointment when he saw that in the meantime the potato had decayed. "Was Father mistaken?" he wondered. When he returned home he told the sad news; but those words were the last he ever uttered. He too died — of the exertion and the disappointment.

A worm of the third generation then crawled out to see it — and he found the potato in an even worse condition than the one his father had seen. It had become entirely waxy. And so the story of the potato became a family tragedy, passed on from one generation to the next.

And then, after many, many generations of worms, a new potato plant, sprouting not merely one but many potatoes, sprang up from the rotten potato. This process of growth, which the worm could not see, was well-known by the farmer who had planted the original potato so many worm-generations ago.

*

Is it a coincidence that Boruch is sitting here with me while I meditate about the meaning of *zorei'a tsᵉdakot matsmi-aḥ yᵉshu'ot*? For there is a connection between Boruch and this idea of help-producing growth. He was named after a little brother of mine, who was born in Westerbork, the *transit-lager* (transit camp) to which Dutch Jews were brought on the way to the concentration camps. He lived only a few weeks, and then he died. Yet even his short life may give us an insight into God's plan of "growth" of salvation.

As I said, my mother *zichrona livracha* (of blessed memory) gave birth to a child in Westerbork, and my parents called him Boruch Neḥemia. Boruch Neḥemia lived less than one month, and died. Why? Why was he not allowed to live longer? And if he was not to live longer, would it not have been better if God had not let him be born at all?

I think that the following may perhaps be an answer:

The commanders of the Westerbork *transit-lager* were so "humane" as to postpone the deportation of the mother of a newly-born child for a certain period. By their rule, a mother of a new infant would be assigned to a later transport, together with her husband and other children; and this happened also in our case. Now, from the transport which was to have taken us originally "to the east," nobody ever returned. Eventually we were deported to Bergen-Belsen. My mother died, but my father and the four children returned from that hell alive.

Thanks to the birth of Boruch Neḥemia?

My mother breast-fed this newborn baby; and then, after the loss of this child, she breast-fed other children, whose own mothers were unable to do so. Thus my mother saved the lives of a number of children.

Thanks to the birth of Boruch Neḥemia?

From this point of view, my father, his children, and other children owe their lives to Boruch Neḥemia. And so will the children of these children, and their grandchildren, until the last of the generations. Was my little brother's short life, thus, not very meaningful?

The Ba'al Shem Tov said that sometimes a soul descends to this world and remains here seventy, eighty years merely to do one single good deed for one other person. How much good Boruch Neḥemia produced in his lifetime of less than one month!

I am convinced that my little brother's life was very meaningful. I am no less convinced that the same reasoning can apply to other children who died at an early age—even if in most cases we cannot see the process that was to evolve by God's plan.

*

Thus it was that on this Friday morning I sang the words *zorei'a tsᵉdakot matsmi-aḥ yᵉshu'ot* while our dear Boruch, the child who was named after Boruch Neḥemia, sat next to me.

That same Friday our little Boruch was hit by a car. He died in the hospital, barely three years old.

Sh^ema, that is Yisrael...

When my wife and I returned from the hospital it was evening: the Shabbat had come. Later that same evening, a friend came to visit us. He had heard the sad news, and though it was a long walk from his house to ours, that had not deterred him. In his attempt to give us solace, he told us that earlier in his life, he too had lost a child.

Yet his words did not penetrate. I had no feelings left. I could not think straight. We just sat there, my wife and I, with only one thought: Boruch...Boruch...Why...? Why...?

In my mind, helplessly, I tried to turn the clock back: I would take care that he did not go outside. Then he would not be hit by that car. Then we would not ever have had to go to the hospital, and he would be snug, asleep.

No, it was no use. It just made no sense. Not long before, I had tried to comfort a woman whose husband was killed in an accident. I had explained to her that she should not blame herself, as she probably did. She had sent her husband shopping, and on his way back he was run over. So she tended to harp on one theme: If she only had not sent him. If she only had asked someone else. Then...then...In this way, I thought, she was blaming herself.

I had tried to argue her out of this reasoning. I
explained to her that her husband would have died at
that very same moment, nevertheless, even if she had
not sent him shopping. His time had come. Death is an
event which God "does not leave to chance." Everything is *b*e*hashgaha p*e*ratit*, everything is planned by
Him to the smallest detail. If we have any awareness of
the reality of God, we understand that such a drastic
event as dying cannot be a matter of random chance.
All this I explained to this woman; and she was
grateful: "You are the first one who has said something
sensible."
Should all this not apply to us as well...?

*

The following day I told our four oldest children, one by
one, of our stark tragedy. "Boruch," I told them, "used
to call himself *tsaddik, tamim v*e*yashar*, and sometimes
he thought that was his name. Well, *Hakadosh-baruch-
hu* loves *tsaddikim*, and He has taken Boruch to
Himself. Boruch is now in Gan Eden."

*

I had often explained to people how Gan Eden should
be perceived. There is more than this world alone. There
are other worlds, other states, other spheres, which are
not material. In those worlds there are also active
beings—various kinds of active beings—among them
angels and *n*e*shamot*, souls.

Before a human is born, he already exists as a soul in these higher worlds. When he is born the soul is connected with a body. And when a person dies, this connection is broken and the soul returns to "the realm above."

*

The *l^evayah* (funeral), the *shiv'a* (seven days of mourning) and all the other rituals of sorrow—I knew that they are important for the survivors as well as for the deceased. That **we** sit *shiv'a* **here** is for the good of the *n^eshama* **there**—just as the Kaddish prayer has a purifying effect on the *n^eshama*.

I decided to do everything as well as I could, to give Boruch all that was in my power to give him **now**. I was entirely occupied by this thought, and I was able to do everything just as it ought to be done. I had no time now to dwell on my sorrow. On other people, I probably made the impression that I had no emotions. But that didn't matter.

Now I suddenly understood the behavior of others who at the time, in similar circumstances, had seemed so unfeeling. Nobody who has not himself gone through this experience—may God spare everyone—can understand this. There are simply two categories of people: those who have had this experience and those who have not.

How can we understand and explain the process of dying? How can we clarify the nature of life after death?

If there is something we cannot understand directly, using a parable can help. In this case, let me use the phenomenon of television.

A person is sitting and watching a program on a television screen. The set has received the program, and it appears clearly on the screen. However, even before it reached the screen, for a fragment of time, the program had already existed in the form of waves sent through the air by the transmitting station.

The operation of television can thus be divided into three parts: (1) the transmitting station; (2) the waves; and (3) the receiver.

Suppose that suddenly for some reason, the person doesn't see the picture anymore. Something goes wrong, and the set no longer shows the program on the screen. That part of the television system has ceased to exist. Yet the other two parts of the system continue to exist. The station continues to transmit and the program is still present in the form of waves, although the man before the set cannot see that. As far as he is concerned the program is gone...

Analogously, I might say that the totality of my person consists of a body *and* a soul *and* a "region" between them. What I feel of myself, how I experience myself, is my body plus "something else." This "something else" is not the soul itself, but the radiation of the soul, the light of the soul as it is received by my body—in thoughts, in feelings. And it is the radiations of the soul that cause the mechanism of my body to function.

Before a child is born it already exists—as a soul. The soul radiates light. The further the light "recedes," the weaker it becomes. That is in fact the meaning of the statement that the soul descends. Not the soul itself descends, but only the light of the soul. At birth the soul makes contact with the body through its light, and the baby comes to life. From this moment on, the person no longer consists of merely two parts—the soul and the light of the soul—but of three. The body has been added.

The intensity of the soul itself is too great to be absorbed by the body. But the intensity of the soul-light is mitigated for earthly existence, and it may also vary during the course of earthly existence: This intensity can increase or decrease. Several factors determine the process.

At the end of a person's earthly existence the contact of the light of the soul with the body is broken. Then the person again consists of its two original parts, the soul and its light. As such, in this state, the person continues to exist. It is now clear that a material event, such as a car accident, cannot terminate the total existence of a person, no more than a bullet can do this.

Here is what the Lubavitcher Rebbe, Rabbi M. M. Schneerson, once wrote to a war widow, in a letter given here in free translation:

The ties between two people, and certainly those between husband and wife, or between parents and children, are chiefly of a spiritual, not of a material, nature. That means that a bullet, a grenade, or a disease can affect the body, but not the spirit or the soul. The physical bond between two persons can be broken by a bullet, but not their spiritual relationship.

The soul of a departed person remains in contact with the members of his family, especially with the most beloved ones. The deceased "knows" what happens here; our grief is his grief and our joy is his joy. If we have the strength to continue living—especially when we, as Jews, live a Jewish life—we give the deceased, who observes all this, a very special experience of happiness.

*

This explanation can help us form a better idea of reincarnation. In a current life, the soul of a human being may have established contact with a body for the first time for earthly existence. But it is also possible that this soul was connected with a body before. In that case, through its radiation, it has absorbed many impressions and a great deal of information, largely positive, certainly, but some undoubtedly negative. The soul must, consequently, pass through a process of *tikkun*, cleansing and repair. This process may occur "above," but it may also take place here. If, by God's will, *tikkun* must take place here, the soul is "reborn," reincarnated.

Judaism does know of reincarnation. True, it is not presented as something to be studied in detail. But it can be important for us to be aware of the fact itself. For it answers many of the questions with which man struggles, such as the dilemma of the meaning of suffering.

*

In *Baderech* we once disccussed the concepts of "Life Hereafter" and "Resurrection of the Dead." We wrote there:

How should we imagine the "Resurrection of the Dead"?

To find an answer, we should realize, first of all, that man is more than body alone; man is a combination of body and soul.

In times of old this was generally accepted. The intuitive awareness of the soul as an independent entity

is as old as man. Of all the "experiences of the soul,"
religious and aesthetic experiences and the ·
consciousness of a self—independent of the body—are
probably the most characteristic aspects of human
perception.

Nineteenth-century materialism tried to explain all
experiences of the soul as phenomena of the brain, as
physical functions, just like breathing and digestion. It
denied that the soul is something "independent" of the
body. As a scientific-philosophical system, this
view—according to which man is merely a
physiologically functioning organism—never had many
adherents. It failed to explain the phenomenon of
"man" in any fully, truly satisfactory manner.
Moreover, such phenomena as telepathy, telekinesis and
bilocation, which have been empirically proven to exist,
are strong arguments for the existence of both body and
soul.

The body receives the "soul-light" and lives by it. When
this light no longer radiates within the body, the
human being is dead–which means that the physical
aspect of his total personality has vanished. His soul,
however, now independent of the body, lives on.

(The physical aspect, however, does not entirely vanish.
A bond continues to exist between the soul and the
remains of the body and/or the place where the body
was buried and the matseva, the tombstone, was
erected. The rituals of shiv'a, sheloshim [the 30 days of

mourning] and other mourning customs, are also related to, and involved with, this continuing bond.)

During his earthly existence a person experiences himself in the first place as a body made alive by the soul.

When a person dies and his body ceases to function, he experiences himself on the level of the soul and the light of the soul, which cannot be observed by us. To us he is "dead"; in reality he lives on in another state.

This other state we call Gan Eden, the Hereafter. It is the state from which, before birth, the soul originally "descended" in order to make contact with the body. And to this state the soul returns after death.

About this state of existence Maimonides writes:

Just as the blind cannot see the gamut of colors and the deaf cannot hear the tone of sound, so the mortal body cannot understand the spiritual joys (attained in the Hereafter) which are eternal and unceasing. These joys have nothing in common with the happiness derived from material things. The essential nature of this heavenly bliss lies in the perception of the Essence of the Creator...in the Hereafter, where our souls become wise with the knowledge of God.

This joy is unknowable, altogether beyond our ability to describe it—and nothing can be compared to it. For us mortal creatures, it is merely possible to speak of it in the words of the prophet which express the wonder of this eternal joy: "How abundant is Your goodness!"

This state too comes eventually to an end, however, when the dead arise and man again becomes an integrally combined entity of soul and body—but a body of an unimaginably higher spiritual quality.

When the days of the Mashiaḥ come—and especially when the dead arise—the world will reach the perfection for which it was created in the beginning.

*At that time the Jewish people shall perceive—even with eyes of flesh and blood—the Essence of the Creator, as we read in Scripture (Isaiah 30:20): "Then shall your Teacher not hide Himself anymore, but your eyes shall see your Teacher." Through this abundant light, which will then be the allotment of Jewry, the darkness of the entire world will be illuminated, as we read in the Holy Writ (Isaiah 40:5): "And the glory of the Lord shall be revealed and **all** flesh will see it together."*

The fact that we cannot form an idea of life in the Hereafter and of the Resurrection of the Dead is elsewhere explained as follows:

The life of the embryo in its mother's womb is entirely different from its life after birth. It is nourished through the umbilical cord, and the circulation of its blood is connected to that of its mother. Its mouth, nose, eyes and ears do not function. Its little arms and legs are folded.

Imagine the unborn baby thinking about life after its embryonic state. Would it be able to form an idea of that life? And would it long for it? It would probably look forward with fear to the moment of its "death," which is in fact the moment of its birth. For its "death"/birth is the passage from one form of life to another. And this transition is so radical that it is impossible for a being in one state to imagine the other.

The same is true of the passage from the earthly state to the "heavenly" mode of existence, and from that to the final state, at the Resurrection of the Dead.

IV

For my wife and me it has been very important that we became familiar with these concepts much earlier. We have not had to begin to believe in them suddenly, under the influence of our present tragic circumstances. Had we begun clutching at these perceptions only now, it could perhaps have been explained as wishful thinking, as the wish becoming father to the thought.

With us this is certainly not the case. The question whether there is life after death has often been put to us, well before the loss of our Boruch — when we could yet never imagine that something like this would ever happen to us. After all, you read about such accidents in the paper, you know that these things occur, but you just don't pay attention. You never really consider that this, Heaven beware, may actually happen to you.

In the days when the future still smiled upon us, we had already read and learned about these matters. We had come to understand that there is a pre-existence and a post-existence in relation to **earthly** life — a "herebefore" and a hereafter. We knew that Boruch had existed before he was born into our family. Perhaps he had already been "on earth" more than once. And now we knew that he lived on in that other, immaterial state.

It is a great comfort to know this: He is still alive.

Yes, he is still alive—it is true—but not here, with us. How we miss him. We want to feel him, kiss him, embrace him—physically. Why was he not allowed to live **here** any longer?

I remember a story I read in the chassidic literature: of a child who lived only two years. When the little boy died, his broken-hearted mother went to see the Ba'al Shem Tov and poured out her heart before him. The Ba'al Shem Tov listened patiently, then explained to her that the *n^eshama* of her child had already descended to this world before. After that earlier incarnation, that previous lifetime on earth, this *n^eshama*, a very special soul, yet had to go through a *tikkun*, a repairing purification. Therefore the *n^eshama* had to be born again in a child. And when the task was completed, at the end of two years, the *n^eshama* returned to "above."

I believe that this must be true of Boruch as well. His task on earth was completed and there was no need for him to continue living here—on earth…just as Boruch Nehemia had completed his task on earth, in the camp of the Nazis. In His infinitely greater wisdom, God arranges that.

All right, agreed: God arranges that. Nonetheless, nonetheless, I wonder: Could the all-powerful God not have arranged this in some other way, without the need to take our child away?

One evening, during the days of the *shiv'a*, someone
tells about Rabban Yohanan ben Zakkai, a Sage of the
Talmud whose son died. "Comfort me," he asked his
disciples.

Rabbi Eliezer spoke up: "Adam lost a son too.
Nevertheless, he found consolation."

But Rabban Yohanan only retorted, "Why do you add to
my sorrow the sorrow of someone else?"

Rabbi Yehoshua spoke in turn: "Job had sons and
daughters, and he lost them all. Nevertheless he found
consolation."

Again Rabban Yohanan only answered, "Why do you
add to my sorrow the sorrow of someone else?"

Then Rabbi Yosse said, "Aharon had two exceptional
sons who both died on the same day. Yet Aharon was
comforted."

This too Rabban Yohanan rejected with the same
words.

Rabbi Simon then rose and spoke: "King David lost a
son, and was nevertheless comforted."

Rabban Yohanan only reacted as before.

Then Rabbi Elazar ben Arach spoke: "Allow me to tell
you this story: A king entrusted one of his subjects with
a precious object, to keep safe for him — and the man
worried incessantly. For he had to return this object to
the king undamaged. Only when he returned the
precious thing to the king intact was he able to give up
his anxiety. You, my teacher, are in the same situation.
You had a son who has left this world without sin. Let
it be a consolation that you have returned to God in a
perfect state what He entrusted to you."

"Elazar, you have comforted me!" Rabban Yoḥanan
said.

*

I wondered why the words of Rabbi Elazar ben Arach
were able to give Rabban Yoḥanan solace and comfort,
while those of the other Sages were not. If you know
that something is part of life, that it happens, that it
has occurred frequently, do you not experience your
pain differently, otherwise than if it had afflicted you
alone? Why, then, did the words of the other Sages have
no effect?

Quite true: such knowledge can change the quality and
nature of your suffering; but this knowledge does not
comfort. Rabbi Elazar, however, gave Rabban Yoḥanan
a different way of looking at the tragic event in his life:
He had not been **deprived** of his son; he had rather
returned him. Rabban Yoḥanan had received his son

as a **loan**; he had not **owned** him. Everything a man thinks he owns, is in fact merely a loan. He may use it, cherish it, but he must know that he may have to return it at any moment.

The same idea is expressed in the story of Bruria, the wife of Rabbi Meir. Their two sons suddenly died on a Shabbat, and the mother laid the bodies in the bedroom. When her husband came home, she said, "A long time ago someone entrusted a precious stone to me for safekeeping. I have kept and cherished that stone carefully. Now the owner has come back. Should I return that precious stone to him?" When Rabbi Meir answered the question in the affirmative, she led him to the bedroom.

The same thought is discussed by Rabbi Schneur Zalman of Liady (founder of Chabad Chassidism) in the fourth part of his renowned work *Tanya*. There was a time when I began to learn this exposition by heart…

My wife and I too will have to absorb this idea: we have not been **deprived** of Boruch; we "only" **gave** him **back**.

V

Many people appear during the *shiv'a*. Visitors keep
coming and going the entire day. In the morning we
have a *minyan*. My wife in particular finds it
comforting that men who usually do not put on *tefillin*,
are doing it now. This provides something of value for
our loss.

In the evening, again, there is a *minyan*. Especially
then our home is full; it is easier for people to come
then, together with many others—to visit a family
during the *shiv'a* alone, is much more difficult, for what
can one say. How can one comfort?

There are people who talk about one thing and another.
They try to keep our minds from our grief, so that for a
while we will not think of what has happened.

They mean well. I am grateful to them for their good
intentions. But I do not want to be diverted. I **want** to
think of Boruch, to see him before me in my mind. For
if you would merely sit here with me, I think, and feel
with me—perhaps without words—or if we talked about
him together, then you would also miss him, and we
would feel the loss together. And only such company in
distress can make our sorrow less. But if people talk of
other things, good as their intentions may be, the pain
remains as deep as it was before they came.

The woman who drove the car which hit our child also
comes to see us—with a friend who had been with her
in the automobile. We understand how difficult this
must be for her. It is very brave of her to gather the
courage to come.

The other visitors, realizing who she is, fall silent. It is
as if they regard her as an enemy, as the murderess of
our child. But we try to put her at ease and tell her that
we do not blame her: for everything is "beshert,"
b^ehashgaḥa p^eratit, foreseen and arranged by God.
Even if she had not driven too fast, Boruch would not
have been with us any more. For his time had evidently
come.

*

I think again of the first Boruch, my little brother who
died when he was less than a month old. The little child
died, along with six million others, only because he was
Jewish. Had he not been a member of a Jewish family,
he would not have perished at the hands of the Nazis.
Since he died solely because of his Jewishness, this
meant that he was taken from this world *al kiddush
haShem*, for the sanctification of God's name.

In this context the thought of Rabbi Joseph Karo comes
to mind. It was revealed to him that he would die *al
kiddush Hashem* at an early age, and he accepted this
fate as a great privilege. Later, however, this privilege
was taken away from him, and Rabbi Joseph Karo

went on to write his famous *Beit Yosef* and the *Shulḥan Aruch*. Yet the great merit he acquired by writing these texts—works used continually to this very day—is still less than the merit of dying *al kiddush haShem*.

*

We are strongly attached to life. If someone's life is in danger, we must do everything possible to save it. Even the laws of Shabbat are set aside for this purpose, if necessary. If the *kohen gadol* (the High Priest), on the point of entering the Holy of Holies on Yom Kippur, were to see a human being in mortal danger, even he—the holiest man of his people in the holiest place in the world at the holiest time of the year—would have to interrupt his sacred service to try to save that life—and even if the chance of success was small.

Why is life here on earth so important?

The reason is that only **here**, in this material world, can the soul fulfill its task through the body. For it is precisely here that God wants a "dwelling place," a setting of action and interaction for His purposes.

This is why we are attached to life. This is why we must do everything to preserve our earthly life and that of others—in order to be able to implement the Divine command, making use of our Divine privilege.

Yet one day we must die. And if we were given the right
to choose how to die, we would probably not realize it
while we live, but after passing over to the other world,
we would know that dying *al kiddush haShem* is the
most sublime way to end our earthly life.

VI

Yet I feel strange inside. Nothing seems to be working right. The normal process of thinking quietly and then reaching a conclusion does not function. And even when I come to some intellectual understanding, I cannot control my feelings.

Oh my God, it hurts so much: Boruch...Boruch...why did you go away?...We miss you so...Let it all be a dream from which I'll wake up soon...It cannot be true...Things like that should not happen...How can a **loving** God allow this?

I believe in God. It is not what people call blind faith. I believe in the Creator in various ways. I **feel** that He exists. And I **understand** that He exists. It is good—and sometimes necessary—to support our faith with rational arguments...especially at a time like this. For I know that parents in similar circumstances have lost their faith. So I find it good to consider again, one by one, the reasons for my belief in God.

Emunah—faith—derives from a verb which also means "to exercise." In *Tehillim*, the Book of Psalms, we read: *ur^e'eh emunah*, "pasture faith"; we must tend and feed our faith. Belief has to be a dynamic activity.

I have often dealt with this subject—in talking to others. I have explained that we believe in a Higher

Power for a variety of reasons. For example: nothing in the world comes into being by itself. That means, as well, that the world in its totality has not come into being by itself. There is a *Generator.*

The more the scientists—biologists, biochemists, ecologists, nuclear physicists, mathematicians—penetrate into the mysteries of the micro- and macro-cosmos, the more they become convinced that this incredibly ingenious system is the work of a *Super-organizer.*

Again, the survival of the Jewish people is a mystery. According to the laws of sociology the Jewish people should have ceased to exist long ago. Over and over again in its history, it has been exposed to powers which should have been able to destroy it spiritually and physically. Nevertheless, in spite of all this, the Jewish people exists, thanks to a *Preserver.*

By such lines of thought we can reach the conclusion that there must be an *Eternal Being,* for otherwise life is incomprehensible and meaningless. And starting from the findings of theoretical physics, we can understand what was already formulated a long time ago in Judaism, and especially by Chassidism—that the *Generator-Super-organizer-Preserver is beyond time and space, and is All-Embracing:*

"Man and matter are not composed of tangible substance, but of entirely elusive processes without a

clear boundary between spirit and matter. Scientifically
it appears that spirit and body, time and space,
universe and atom are all aspects of one Reality which
to an ever increasing degree appears to be one great
Thought."

This is a scientific formulation of what we have
expressed over the centuries in the words *haShem
ehad*—God is One.

*

Actually, everybody is a believer. Even those who claim
to have no faith, are believers. For "to believe" means
to accept and acknowledge something that cannot be
known. There **are** things in the world which cannot be
known—or can be known only partially. But we do
accept their existence. For we understand that human
reason is not the only criterion for deciding whether
something exists or not. And we accept its existence,
not because we can prove it absolutely, but because it is
very plausible, and indeed evident, beyond denial.
In this manner reason may go far to make the existence
of God plausible and highly probable. It is extremely
improbable that God does **not** exist.

People who deny His existence say that they do not
believe. But this formulation is simply wrong. They **do**
believe: They believe in the non-existence of God.
And just as I believe in His existence and try to make

this plausible and highly probable—virtually evident—so a person who believes in the Creator's non-existence must equally find ways to support his view with ironclad arguments. He too must explain the origin and organization of the world; he too must find causes for the survival of the Jewish people. He cannot evade this task.

It is not enough for him to declare that science **will eventually** explain all this. And if he does declare this, he merely shows that in this way he, too, is a believer.

*

I believe in God. And that is precisely why I ask how a loving God could allow such a dreadful, terrible thing to happen—to wrench from me a child who was part of my heart. If I did not believe in God, ḥas veshalom (perish the thought), I would not be surprised that there is so much suffering in the world. For if He did not exist, ḥas veshalom, the world would be a jungle in which the might of the strongest rules, where only the Darwin's laws apply: struggle for life, survival of the fittest.

But I do believe in God. And for this reason I grope and seek an answer. I understand that a creature can never see "through the eyes" of the Creator. The powers of every creature are limited; he is only three-dimensional, subject to the limitations of time and space. How can a creature then hope to see things as God "sees" them!

I understand—with my reason—that everything He does is good, that it cannot be different. Sometimes we think that we recognize His goodness. And when we do not recognize it, we must accept that nevertheless, we are encountering goodness—**hidden** goodness.

Rabbi Shneur Zalman of Liady discusses this concept of hidden goodness in the first part of his *Tanya*, a major classic of chassidic thought. He develops it out of an earlier teaching that we have in the Mishna. And elsewhere in chassidic literature the phenomenon of hidden goodness is clarified in a parable:

Let us imagine a wise and just person, without defects of character, who is doing his best to raise his family. He is a good, loving father—and yet, one day, he decides to berate and chastise his son. Of one thing we may be sure: It is an expression of love: *yissurim mé-ahavah*. The father must have his reasons for doing this, in this way, out of love for his son—a love that has its roots in his deepest inner self. His love may be so deeply felt that it cannot be expressed openly, in a revealed form.

A sensible son will do his best to understand it, with his intellect—and he will not revolt against his father. Perhaps, after having given it some thought, he will even perceive the chastisement as good.

*

Yet how difficult this is for a common human being.
And nevertheless there have been people who were able
to do it—and there still are. My mind turns to Rabbi
Zyshe of Anipoli, a man who lived in the most
appalling conditions, and still did not ever regard his
sufferings as misery. In spite of his poverty, the bitter
cold of winter, his hunger and other sources of
wretchedness, he declared that he had never
experienced distress.

I think of the Hassidim who sang *Ani ma'amin* on
their way to the gas chamber. *Ani ma'amin*—I believe
in perfect faith; *im kol zeh*—in spite of everything: In
spite of the never-ending persecutions, expulsions,
pogroms and gas chambers, I believe that all this has
been for the good, has been in preparation for the
coming of Mashiah, for the final messianic
Redemption of the world. Thus Hassidim knew how to
sing in sorrow.

I think of those exceptional Russian Jews who,
notwithstanding all the hardship of their long
imprisonment in the work camps, found it a matter of
course never to work on Shabbat and Yom Tov, never
to eat *treif*, forbidden food.

And I think of their wives, who did everything to
observe the commandments of family purity and the
ritual bath. Amid bewildering misery and pain, they
regarded everything as expressions of God's goodness.

Others before me found a way to take this path.

*

These thoughts were reflected in one issue of *Baderech*:

*We must learn to see our personal life as part of a great whole: Our joy, our suffering become meaningful only if we perceive them in the context of history—the history of our people and of mankind at large. When we see our own lives as links in the long chain of the generations, the importance of our own experiences becomes muted and relative. In this way our personal experiences are elevated to the level of universal experience; they are raised from private, personal suffering to form part of ongoing human life in the world. If in his supreme need a man can say Sh*ᵉ*ma Yisrael, if a mourner can praise God's holiness in the Kaddish prayer, his personal suffering assumes a wider perspective and becomes thereby somewhat easier to bear.*

How can we judge what is good or bad for an individual? How can we perceive the constellation of forces through which God guides the ongoing course of indivduals and nations?

This is the trend of the answer that the Creator gives Job in a series of powerful rhetorical questions, in the last chapters of the great biblical book that bears his name.

In his book Jom Jom, *Dr. D. Hausdorff of Rotterdam
gives a free summary of these chapters:*

*"Do you really think, Job, that you can understand
everything? Man is so small, he has such a small
intellect, that he simply cannot understand everything
God does.*

Did you happen to create the world, Job?

*Do you determine the orbit of the sun and the moon and
the stars?*

*Do you see to it that animals in this world receive their
food on time?*

*Do you make the thunder roll and the lightning flash
through the sky?*

*Should a man not be humble, then, and realize that he
can often not understand the Almighty and All-wise
God?"*

*He confronts Job with his littleness against the
backdrop of both inanimate and living nature, He
makes Job realize man's inability to understand the
deeper ground of his suffering. But God also condemns
the simple "explanation" of Job's friends that suffering
is always a punishment for one's sins.*

*

It is, of course, true that God rewards and punishes. He reacts in His way to man's behavior. When misery befalls a person, Heaven forbid, he should therefore examine himself to see if and how it is his own fault. Sometimes he will find an answer, but more often he will not. Why not? Because God wants us to act out of our own free will. The choice between good and evil that we have to make, over and over again, must be made freely, not out of coercion. If I receive a reward immediately after having performed a good deed, I shall continue to perform this deed. But this is no longer truly free will.

Similarly, if I am punished immediately after having done something bad, I am not likely to do it again. But it will be on account of fear, not by my own perfectly free choice.

God "**must**" therefore give His reward and punishment in hidden ways. We are not permitted to see what was the cause of what. For this reason He may reward or punish us only after many years. Or it may even be in "heaven," in life after death; or in a new earthly life after this life; or immediately, but **in hidden ways**.

*

Actually, His goodness can be seen in nature. We can perceive His care for all creatures, from the smallest to the biggest. There is the maternal instinct He has planted in animals. There are the provisions He made

for every creature to obtain its food — and the species
live on.

Yet this Divine love too is often hidden, not always
visible. A friend of mine, a biologist, made that clear to
us in a letter of condolence that he sent us:

*"I heard what happened, and I grieved for you. Now, at
the moment, I have been walking here in the greatness
of God's nature. It is so infinitely great, so perfect — and
yet sometimes so cruel, as we see it. The birds of the
meadows are numerous here, in a variety of species.
They have their young now. You see them coming along
the range of dunes, the gulls, dazzlingly white against
the blue sky. The meadow birds, the parents, fly up with
loud cries of alarm, in a desperate attempt to protect
their young. But this morning, as so often before, I saw
how things went wrong. A young bird, still so small, so
very immature, was carried away by a predator while
the parent birds remained behind, helpless. All their
care, all those days of patient attention and work had
been in vain. All at once it became clear that it had
been wasted.*

*"What moves me most of all is the parents' tragic flight
back to their now empty parcel of meadow, chosen and
protected with so much care — all in vain...*

*"And yet every year again it is spring, and the meadow
birds obey, as a matter of course, an inner urge.
Jubilant in their courting flight, they hatch their eggs*

once more in cleverly hidden nests, tending and bringing up their young, as if no stark tragedy had ever happened. And the strong, dazzlingly white messengers of God, hovering above them in graceful flight, choose their innocent prey according to incomprehensible laws. We watch, and we wonder...

"I am with you in your brave acceptance and endurance. How can we judge? There is no blind fate, no hand of destiny which strikes blindly, although it is not given to us to see things in their broad connection. In spirit I am with you in your brave faith that all is for the good. And being only human, I walk here in God's great nature and am bewildered by what I see..."

*

May the Almighty grant my wife and me the ability to accept our loss as a manifestation of His goodness. May we at least be able to accept it **intellectually**; and with time may our intellect help our **feelings** to accept it too, and thereby carry on with life.

Postscript

Such were my reflections after God took my son Boruch back. Time has passed. Unimaginable as it may have seemed at the time, it has again become possible to laugh and feel joy, although differently. The wound has healed; but a scar remains.

I have committed all this to writing and exposed my feelings, for in my work as a rabbi, I have come to realize that it can be helpful. Much of what is written here was said in conversation with others—people who knew that the time of their death was near, or people who had suffered a heavy personal loss.

Death remains, inevitably, a part of life. It is therefore important to learn of a view of life which makes it possible to alleviate the pain that dying and death can cause.

Through these reflections I have tried to explain the singing in sorrow of so many millions of Jewish men and women—young and old, learned and illiterate, rich and poor—who kept their faith in God, in spite of all they went through during the Crusades, the Spanish Inquisition, the pogroms, in the camps of Hitler and Stalin—in the unnumbered chapters of Jewish martyrdom.

Without attempting to be exhaustive, I have tried to formulate answers—especially those based on Chabad Chassidism—to the old question of the meaning of suffering. It is a question to which so many could not and cannot find a positive answer, because they do not know of such a Jewish philosophy of life. And it is a question which, unfortunately, has remained unanswered in too many recent publications about the suffering of the Jews in World War II.

May the Almighty spare us further suffering, and may He grant us to witness His **visible** goodness.

GLOSSARY

Explanation of Hebrew terms

Al kiddush Hashem	— For the sanctification of God's Name
(Be)hashgaha peratit	— (By) God's Providence in even the smallest events
Beracha	— Blessing
Has veshalom	— Heaven forbid!
Gan Eden	— The Garden of Eden, Paradise
Hakadosh-Baruch-Hu	— The Holy One, praised be He
Kaddish	— The traditional prayer in which God's greatness and encompassing might are praised
Levayah	— The accompaniment of a departed person to his grave
Mikveh	— Ritual bath for obtaining spiritual cleanness
Minyan	— Quorum of ten males (at least 13 years old) required for congregational prayers
Mishna	— Compilation of the laws in the Oral Torah, as given by God on Mount Sinai
Neshama	— Soul
Rosh Hashana	— The Jewish New Year
Shiv'a	— The seven days of mourning after the funeral
Shul	— Synagogue
Shulhan Aruch	— Jewish code of law for daily use
Tefillin	— Phylacteries, put on for the weekday morning prayer
Tikkun	— Purification of the soul
Torah	— The Pentateuch, the first part of the Hebrew Bible (Tanach)

Tsaddik tamim v^{e}yashar	—	Righteous, innocent and honest
Yissurim mé-ahavah	—	Chastisement out of love
Yom Kippur	—	Day of Atonement
Yom Tov	—	Religious holiday